THE WAR AT HOME

BY TAMMY ZAMBO

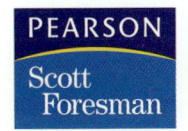

Editorial Offices: Glenview, Illinois • Parsippany, New Jersey • New York, New York
Sales Offices: Needham, Massachusetts • Duluth, Georgia • Glenview, Illinois
Coppell, Texas • Sacramento, California • Mesa, Arizona

The Home Front

World War II was a conflict between the Allies and the Axis powers. In the United States a lot of attention was given to the troops who were fighting the war. However, the United States could not have helped the Allies win the war without the hard work of the government, businesses, and millions of everyday people on the home front.

Women in the Military

After the bombing of Pearl Harbor, Hawaii, on December 7, 1941, the military needed millions of people to send into battle. Many Americans volunteered. Others had to serve because of the draft. All of these people, however, were men. Women were not allowed to serve on the battlefield and were not drafted.

The military had a problem, though. Because a large number of men were sent to fight overseas, many important military positions on the home front were empty. The military created units in which women could sign up to fill the empty positions.

Women signed up to work for every branch of the military. Women in the army and navy nurse corps traveled all over the world to nurse wounded soldiers and sailors. Women pilots who joined the Women Airforce Service Pilots (WASP) flew all types of planes, including fighters and bombers. Women in the Coast Guard Women's Reserve (known as SPARS) set up parachutes and coded and decoded messages sent to ships. By the end of the war, more than 244,000 women had served in the military.

Women pilots in the Women Airforce Service Pilots (WASP) flew all kinds of planes during the war.

Civilian Defense Volunteers

A new agency called the Office of Civilian Defense (OCD) encouraged civilians, or people not serving in the military, to volunteer. Volunteers called wardens conducted alarm drills and made sure that people observed **blackouts**. A blackout is when lights are turned off to hide targets from the enemy during an air raid at night.

Many civilian pilots volunteered for the Civil Air Patrol (CAP). They flew members of the military, blood supplies, and mail from place to place in their own planes.

Aircraft and other war materials were built on assembly lines, just as cars had been during peacetime.

Changes in Business

Troops fighting the war needed an enormous amount of equipment and supplies. All across the country, factories made changes to produce these goods. Automobile factories made military vehicles, airplanes, and weapons instead of cars. Some aircraft parts were built by a washing machine company. A maker of typewriters made rifles during the war.

These business changes created millions of new jobs that paid well. People everywhere—over fifteen million altogether—moved to new places to fill these jobs. The United States had never experienced so many people moving at once. A severe housing shortage developed in many cities as newcomers arrived.

Overcrowded boardinghouses were common in boomtowns.

Boomtowns

The population rose quickly in towns where shipyards, factories, and military bases were located. For this reason, they were called boomtowns. Housing in boomtowns was in short supply. People took in boarders, which meant that they rented spare rooms in their homes to strangers. Some people set up trailers or tents, and some even slept in parked cars.

The community of Willow Run, Michigan, grew rapidly when a new aircraft factory opened there. Eventually this factory would employ more than forty thousand people. To house its giant assembly line, the factory at Willow Run was one mile long! Another aircraft factory at Fort Worth, Texas, was so large that supervisors rode bicycles inside the building in order to visit different parts of the factory.

This poster of Rosie the Riveter, and others like it, urged women to go to work for the war effort.

Working Women

Before the war, most women stayed home to care for their families. When millions of men left their jobs to serve overseas in the military, many jobs were vacant. The government needed women to work for the war effort.

More than six million women went to work for their country. They were inspired by billboards and posters featuring images such as Rosie the Riveter. They were eager to help the war effort, and they worked hard in their new jobs.

By 1944, women were 36 percent of the paid workforce. They helped the Allies win the war. Yet women were paid 40 percent less than men for working in the same jobs. In addition, most women lost their jobs when men came home at the end of the war.

Many women joined the workforce, as in this weapons factory.

Japanese American families wait for a bus to take them to an internment camp.

The Internment Camps

Americans pulled together to win the war. For many people, however, pulling together meant treating other Americans differently. After Japan bombed the United States naval base at Pearl Harbor, many people felt that Japanese Americans could not be trusted. They were afraid that some Japanese Americans might work as spies and give important information to the Japanese government. The United States government shared this fear. In February 1942, President Franklin Roosevelt signed an order which allowed United States Army commanders to order the removal of Japanese Americans from the West Coast of the United States.

Shortly afterwards, about 120,000 Japanese Americans had to leave their homes and businesses. They were taken to **internment** camps built especially as housing units for Japanese Americans. The crowded camps were surrounded by barbed wire and guarded by soldiers.

Despite the harsh way they were treated, Japanese Americans were very patriotic. Many Japanese American men served in the United States Army during the war. The government released Japanese Americans over time and then began to close the camps in early 1945.

Japanese Americans lived in assembly centers while the internment camps were being built.

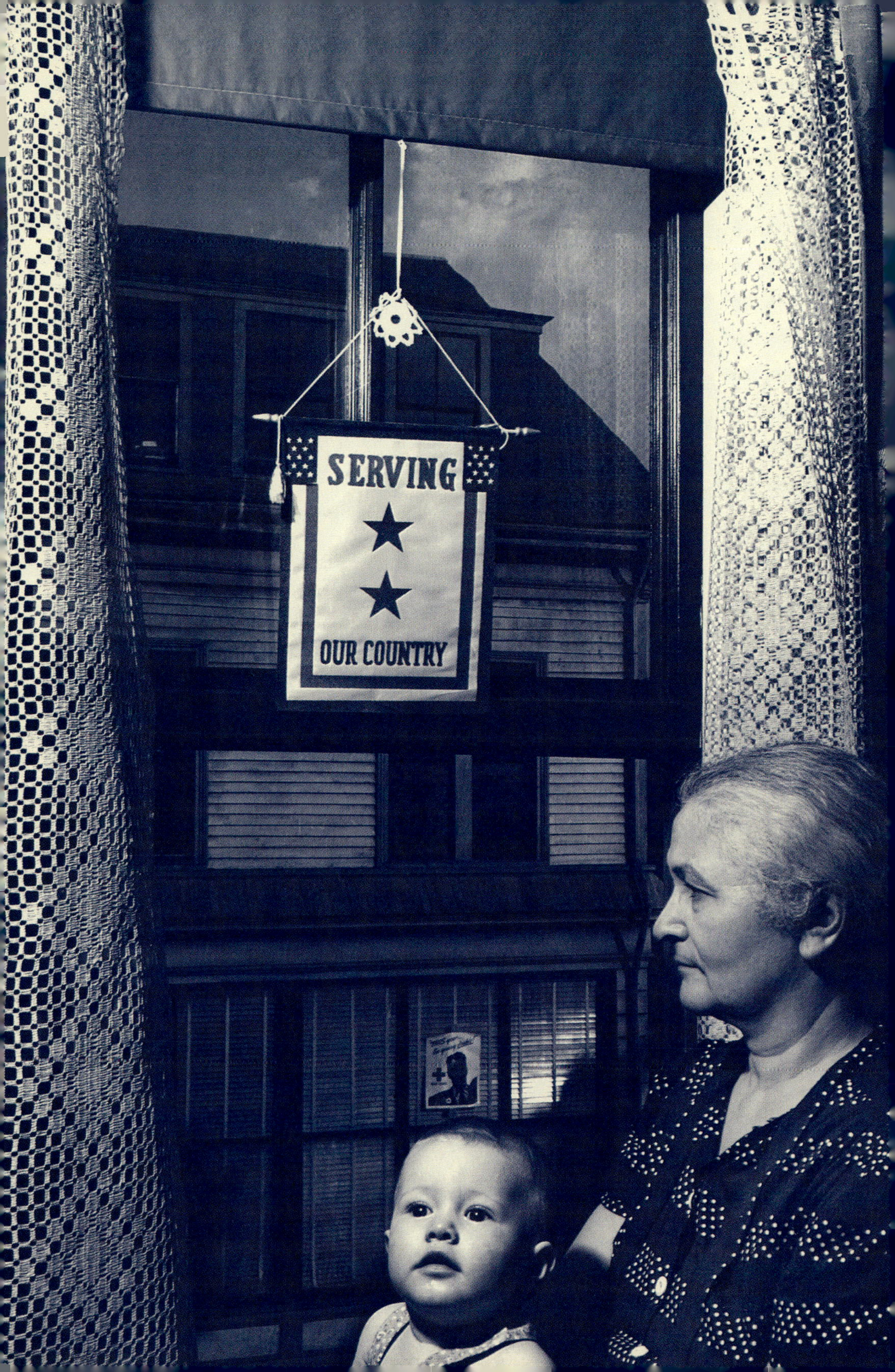
SERVING
OUR COUNTRY

Home-Front Life

Every day Americans were reminded of the war by shortages and **rationing**. Metal was used to build military equipment and weapons, so bicycles were not produced. Automobile factories were involved in war production, so new cars were not available.

Sugar, coffee, butter, cheese, and meat were rationed so that everyone got some but no one got too much. Every family used ration stamps to buy certain products.

To help feed their families, many people planted victory gardens. These gardens produced more than one-third of the vegetables eaten in the United States.

Gasoline was also rationed, so Americans started using different kinds of transportation. Walking and carpooling became common. For longer trips, people took trains. Frequently, though, families simply stayed at home.

People also wrote letters often, especially if a family member was in the military. Families hung a banner in the window with blue stars to show how many family members were fighting in the war. If one of them died, the blue star would be replaced with a gold one.

The banner shows how many family members are serving in the military.

Teenagers' lives changed dramatically when many of them went to work in factories during the war.

Children Do Their Part

Children joined the war effort too. Many of them organized scrap drives. They collected paper, metal cans, and rubber tires from people in their neighborhoods. They also donated their own metal toys and foil that they had saved from packages of gum. These items were recycled and used to make goods for the war.

A great number of teenagers worked in factories and on farms, just as adults did. Nearly three million girls and boys were working by 1943.

Helping to Win the War

Millions of Americans worked hard on the home front in World War II. Daily life for nearly everyone changed. However, people found comfort in the thought that they were helping men and women in the military. They thought their efforts were helping to win the war, and that was what mattered most.

Children often organized drives to recycle scrap rubber and metal.

Glossary

blackout turning out lights to hide targets from an enemy during an air raid at night or from submarines offshore

internment holding and limiting the movement of people during wartime

rationing government limiting the amount of food and other goods each person can buy